Cardinal

in the

Eastern

White

Cedar

Cardinal

in the

Eastern

White

Cedar

ROO BORSON

McClelland & Stewart

Library and Archives Canada Cataloguing in Publication

Borson, Roo, 1952–, author
Cardinal in the eastern white cedar / Roo Borson.

Poems.
Issued in print and electronic formats.
ISBN 978-0-7710-1224-2 (paperback). – ISBN 978-0-7710-1226-6 (epub)

I. Title.

PS8553.O736C37 2017   C811'.6   C2016-904535-8
                                      C2016-904536-6

Published simultaneously in the United States of America
by McClelland & Stewart, a Penguin Random House Company

Library of Congress Control Number is available upon request

ISBN: 978-0-7710-1224-2
ebook ISBN: 978-0-7710-1226-6

Typeset in Aldus by M&S, Toronto
Printed and bound in the USA

McClelland & Stewart,
a division of Penguin Random House Canada Limited,
a Penguin Random House Company
www.penguinrandomhouse.ca

1 2 3 4 5   21 20 19 18 17

CONTENTS

PAINTED

GARDEN

On the second floor of the Palazzo Massimo museum in Rome are the frescoes of a "painted garden," salvaged from the Villa of Livia. These frescoes once decorated the walls of a dining room built partway underground for coolness in the heat of summer. Livia (58 BCE–29 CE) was the wife of Augustus Caesar, emperor of Rome, and a major political figure in her own right. Seemingly alive with numerous birds, flowering plants, and fruiting trees, the garden comes across as intimately familiar, two thousand years being a brief span in the evolutionary history of the oak, pine, or quince. The room in which the frescoes are housed has been equipped with an ingenious variable lighting system, one designed to mimic the path once taken by daylight as it traversed the paintings from dawn to dusk.

I

Cured of ambition and lonely for the old music
in my sixty-third year I came down
from the hills and into town,

past the sour-faced monk selling honey,
and the dazzled bees
half-dozing as they browsed

the low-growing wild herbs
and shades of woodland flowers
among the crypts,

listening for a music few might bother hearing,
inhuman nearly, passing by gelati palaces, past ranks of calfskin
books, long trays of lemon ravioli set out on display,

to join the throngs: each led by a flag, or tassel,
an umbrella or false flower held high
not as the standards once borne into battle

to organize the troops, but to distinguish
the otherwise more or less continuous groups
funnelling into side-streets

to tour the sights, where each day dawns
with bells
and each grudgingly-arrived-at evening ends

4

unready to depart
from the kindness of the sun,
for a future which is the present

that would carry on without us –
as long panels of light are seen to pass,
and farm fields,

from the windows of the passing train
where I rejoined my friends. Janice
the outlasting, who would sit

on a mountain of shards
sorting shards, Andy in a cloud of invisible mentors
recovered from among the dead,

and Kim, whose questionable equanimity
would keep us sane. Then, stepping
from the train, we were in Rome.

Each spring
mirrors the one before,
pre-owned by those now gone from here,

but this was late summer, full-fledged, fully formed,
when the spirits are well-hidden among the leaves.
Thus we dispersed. Janice to her mountain,

keeping watch for a sign
from the last good emperor,
Andy to the museums, holding concourse with the past,

and we two, with the rest of the tourists, to the Baths
of Caracalla, which are dry. Bathed in sunlight,
flitting with speechless birds, the mosaics

still vivid in corners, along edges,
a lost city of arches, geometric pools,
the odd architrave of reddish travertine

melting in sun and rain, now worn bare
to a natural, occasional architecture, made
neither by slaves nor paid labourers

but by the sedimentary labour
of mineral springs alone. Anonymous
as all works and names will one day be,

when those who knew them are themselves unknown.
Afterwards we relaxed in the adjoining grounds
where cats and cat cousins were stalking

the ruins. Two brothers, striped,
well-equipped in eye and claw,
communicating with a look and a glance,

stole from hedge to hedge to hedge in tandem,
undissuadable, disinterested
in anything not of that realm.

Ancient history, the scintillating whiskers of a mole –
what didn't belong to them? All encompassed
by that unimpeachable twin gaze, that martial valour –

that martial valour, twinned – calling on me to learn,
perhaps mistakenly, however late in life,
from my own kind.

Long roads lead to Rome,
straight-sided, presided over
by dark, sculptural pines, regal,

seen nowhere else but in the empire
of a city forever making symbols of itself,
symbols out of living beings.

This we found out soon enough, the four of us,
meeting as planned outside the Colosseum,
standing, amidst the streaming tour groups,

graven to the spot, while in a cleared space
just in front of us, a tall long-legged spotted gull
lifted and let drop, lifted and let drop

a young crow, its wings unfurling in the lifting,
snapping shut like a fan as it fell,
repeatedly, so little meat to cling to,

while a third bird, this a carrion crow, said Andy,
with its mouth agape, waited for the gull to tire
so it could eat its young.

A scene like this might once have been engraved and printed
on a million-lire note. None but us had stopped or noticed.
Espressos, panini, then on to the epigraphy museum,

where form and idea are preserved equally –
the letter *F* (for fame, fortune, the future)
turned on its head and backwards, like that crow, by Claudius,

grandson of Livia and last known speaker of Etruscan,
whose innovations (even this) would be reversed by history,
i.e., imperial edict, failing to outlive his reign.

Next: a pilgrimage, this to the Capitoline. There, when at length
the two of us, first Kim then I, turned from the marble casket lid, its
two dogs lying in repose, we found a tableau

laid before us: Janice, face raised, standing, silent, and before her,
seated on horseback, arm likewise raised, Marcus Aurelius, that
line between the living and the dead – and I began to understand then

something of what I've heard before, whenever she says his name,
in that soft Winnipeg accent, annexed to actual joy.
In my mind I still see her there.

The strangest thing about this kind of life
might be its strangeness, which must be taken for granted
in order to live. This much I had already taken for granted,

taken for granted and forgotten that is, as Andy, Kim, and I entered
that painted garden, one room only, restored from the Villa of Livia.
Empress, poisoner, author of wrath and wrongness,

artist who painted real figs with a tainted brush,
and would murder her husband for her child
then kill the child. No wonder poor Claudius

stuttered in the presence of trouble –
and trouble was always in Rome,
though as usual little can be known for certain.

Half tomb, half summer dining room, sequestered
half-underground in deepest heat, the cool frescoed walls
still hold, suspended, flowers, pine boughs, birds

of all kinds, acanthus, holm oaks –
as though newly reissued from the book of gone things.
These were, as I could see, and yet were not, the flowers

of the outer world – were not, and yet were, signatures.
Not life, but life in the ruins of sunlight
silenced into paint. Three hours might have passed.

Three thousand summers. The delicately rendered birds
would hardly sing in any case, in an empire that exalts
heavy-handed themes and major rhymes. By now it was well

past time – past time to go find Janice, who was waiting for us
in a state of high excitement, down from the dig, having found it
spelled out there, among the unmarked shards, indelible, so no one

could doubt its provenance: AURELIO. The last good emperor. Her
Marcus Aurelius. Andy was first. A quick hug, sharing that evident joy.
Then Kim, who knows the weeks by which my life is shortened

are those without him. After that, everything went into memory.
Like the cats, we were transfixed to the unfolding moment:
drinking local beer, eating fried zucchini blossoms and seafood

fresh off the boats, watching the stragglers, late in,
dock with the sunset.
Our last night was spent on the Tiber.

V

Not then, but twenty years before. Andy had said,
If you're in Florence, cross the river, walk uphill.
You'll find it there. San Miniato.

We entered, Kim and I, just as the monks began
the vespers, each high pure note of the countertenor
summoning the lower voices, call and answer

interweaving in a vocal brocade of unassimilable resonance
some evanescent thread of tenderness, spun of metallic gold.
The climb had been tiring in that heat; I hardly knew where I was,

let alone that such music like life itself must be improvised
every moment and would never be heard again.
In some way that is still unclear I stayed in those hills,

waiting those twenty years until my body returned for me,
accompanied by friends. Just there, Andy (our guide)
would say, the house where Dante lived, and here his Beatrice,

on a live street, in the real city of Firenze.
And if those voices and particular music are gone,
and instead a faint tape is playing and replaying

behind the sour-faced monk dispensing honeys – orange blossom
or acacia – to the occasional unworthy tourist,
I can still look out from that hill as though onto my native place.

There, a Franciscan in robes with a rope for a belt
is strolling the streets as spring arrives in its mirroring
newness, in which daphne, narcissus, and jasmine shed

their individual scents. Janice, Andy, Kim.
If there is a tomb for me it will be in that mirror.
A poetry of the morning turns into the poetry of evening,

as these needlessly logical slip-knots in thought, sound,
and sense are tied and tirelessly untied in semi-darkness.
Before the day ends, I can hear Kim saying

with his usual equanimity, balanced between worlds,
let's leave this place,
and go out again into the daylight with our friends –

go out
while our closest star, the only sun that is our own,
is still shining.

PUTTING A SEAL

ON SPEECH

AND

AN END

TO WANDERING

A SIDEWAYS SPRING

A sideways spring
rain and petals fly
polka-dotting the roofs

Finally the rains end
clouds on the march
snails on the march

The furnace carries on no matter what
deep midnight
winter mind

Wave upon wave lapping the stones
the colour of her eyes
not once forgotten

Shadowrange on shadowrange
playing hide-and-seek
fog and the mountain

In the cirque last year
last remnants of snow
feeding the wild mountain pinks

The bay and its islands
not much else to say
another master of the form

Morning dew
whoever thought to plant
wild strawberries on the graves

Wind in the rafters
a carpenter ant
enters the tree's heart

Having to state my occupation
for the official issuing visas
just another tousle-haired old poet

Round and round the muddy pond
the stew of footprints
neither goose nor human

Everyone's heading home in summer darkness
lightning's fanfare
and the refrigerator strikes up a tune

Still emanating whiteness
blossoms at dusk
sound of insect sounds

Rain's monologue
beneath the lamp
who could be sad just reading all day

In France
even the melons look back at you
in French

Slumped in a chair with a bowl of cherries
hot July night
nothing on but moonlight

Spider in the teapot
moth in the bedclothes
unanswered letters on the table in the house

Wrested from sleep
a cat in the sullen grass
at summer's end

At summer's end
another cat, more sullen grass
another view of the bay

The book tilting in your hands
the words leave off
go through that door

Small black dog
barking at evening
so autumn begins

Dull irreconcilable lettering, oblique insignia
borne aloft, these backlit beings of the dawn
escaped from sleep and too-long-stored provisions
into daylight, only to land, half-shadowed,
on a tuft of wild celery,
or the swaying caraway
that crowds the shack door already
wounded with the scratching of raspberry canes,
no longer tended and run riot,
or one will settle
on the mild midwinter sheen of apple bark,
there to become an emblem
of a fragile, muted, easily unlimbed flight
through forest and clear-cut, troughs and chasms
of airborne dust upon which history rests
then founders, leaving their young
cloistered amid millet, wool, and
walnut shells, there to devour
food and cloth, compelling us, come
unexpectedly upon them,
to step witless and naked once more
as into a dream, a dream
whose logic remains
always just beyond our reach,
yet intricately signifying nonetheless,
as the surprise that caraway
is the stereoisomer of spearmint
signifies, or the intertwining songs of extinct species,
memorized and recited in the extemporaneous

song of the lyrebird, signify. Thus are moths
the cloth of dreams,
in a tailor's book of antique fabric samples,
dotted, streaked, or plain,
or else some mauve astonished plaid
excised with pinking shears,
each sample oblong, nearly square,
and pasted in the book of dusk.
Unlike butterflies,
which fill the garden at the height of summer,
jewelled noonday dawdlers
that travel and alight,
travel and alight at will,
basking in sunlight,
sipping nectars, upright,
these their greyer cousins
are sworn to feast in ulterior light,
never far from mother's satin gowns
embalmed in mothballs
(not-quite-signifying death),
fledglings whose fractured flight,
which turns up, in its wake
over the blackened ground,
milkweed and willowherb, is freighted,
first to rise from ash – these beings
forever laid open to the same two pages,
baring, bearing, or disclosing, as if in a dream,
what is written there: truth, pledge, plight, moth –
unreadable book that will not close.

ONE

Every Tuesday at 4 p.m.
he would come to me, one
of the company of the dead, familiar,
only now in Montreal, in winter;
it would be snowing wonderfully;
I would order a coffee and a sandwich;
but it had to be a Tuesday,
and at 4 p.m., and Montreal,
and then, and only then,
he'd come to me.
And because I had a body,
and now he did not,
this one among the company of the dead,
whom I had known, and thought,
though without thinking, always to be present,
and because I had grown used to it,
I'd order a coffee,
anywhere on earth I'd order a sandwich,
but it had to be a Tuesday, and at 4 p.m.,
in Montreal, and snowing wonderfully,
and then, and only then,
he'd come to me.
I'd order the sandwich and the coffee
as if with my body his might
eat again, and drink, and see;
it would be snowing, wonderfully;
and though it could have been a Wednesday,
in Los Angeles, say, at noon, under the numbing sun,
on the street where he was raised,

where we would sometimes
go when I was young, this is how he came to me:
on Tuesdays, and at 4 p.m., in Montreal,
all that winter, until finally
that winter, with its wonderful
continuously falling snow,
and with it, too, my time in Montreal
were drawing to an end, no matter how much
I'd grown used to it, he went with the snow
and did not return, whether on Tuesday,
or Wednesday, or anywhere,
for it was only there that he would come,
and then, in Montreal, on Tuesday,
just at 4 p.m., while it was snowing wonderfully,
that one among the company of the dead.

As spring insinuates all things into being,
reed, blossom, the early starling's coat of many colours,
and with snow and rain in equal measure, so
summer will come with horse-headed clouds,
the golden legs of the wasp, and creeping jenny
bees look into as into the leaves of a living book.
Such summers' evenings' city lights reprise
in sequence something of the starling's speckled coat,
which darkens into autumn. Autumn, which adores
the varying hare, the wooden maps and silver
forests wherein winters yet to come prepare
all things to be unmade: the horse as the horse chestnut,
the harebell as the hare – till one dry stalk
sloughs off its snow. So ends, at least, this world of thought.

All that spring
the spring had not yet come,
and then at last

the errant petals,
falling everywhere –
the sight of petals

fallen from your hair.
As if some other errand
called to them –

such whiteness, pinkness,
whether born out of spring's lateness,
or in error,

or to summon to that
sudden sky all of blueness:
your eyes.

In the basement of a basement, below stairs,
far below the living city,
hidden from the wheeling world and its stars,

among early fortifications and domestic works,
dye vats, urns, wheels, coins,
still sinking toward that central fire

burning since near the beginnings of the universe:
a row of alabaster heads, unearthed. Citizens
of that once prosperous Roman city on whom

fame was not to be conferred by words,
the flesh made other – likeness of the
mother in the son or father in the daughter: stone –

that those unborn and yet to come
might one day know that countenance.
Touring the underground, among things

gone and yet unvanished, scentless clay
and rootless branchings of the past,
the scoured planks underfoot.

And afterwards, the elevator up,
then further stairs,
and out into the daylight,

where Columbus knelt before a king and queen,
head bowed,
proclaiming grand deeds to the great men

– there assembled and long since forgotten –
of a land where
centuries later many millions would be born.

The horses of North Adelaide are rarely there,
whether in baking sun or steaming rain.
A space of gum-tree shade and emptiness,
lit by the shriek of rainbow lorikeets.
This is a hard ground, broken sun
and biting ants, a violent colonial
history. I've seen the Melbourne hail
and Sydney sleet, tufts of button grass
rising, on a December morning, early,
out of the Tasmanian mist.
Here in this paddock once,
at what was then deemed an acceptable remove,
people were herded, penned up
together – like so many aging horses,
worn out from their labours and of little value.
Now only the horses of North Adelaide
are to be seen, if only on occasion,
tucked into a corner of the field,
glimpsed now and then off in the distance,
between the gum trunks,
ridden by the descendants of the lords and masters
of that time – whether in baking sun or steaming rain,
the marvellous horses of North Adelaide.

And if you should see, along the way, a flock,
or pecking order, a plethora, surfeit, or transubstantiation
of ibises along the river, along the new grass
of the river's banks now that it is autumn and the leaves
are climbing the air – and if you should see them,
a sustainability, or accommodation, of ibises, there
where you are walking, it means that I am thinking
of you, among the narrow faces and arced black beaks
grazing along the river where you are walking not thinking
of anything much, yet counting the ibises as you go, because
you will tell me their number later, and this number will match
the number that you saw, all fifty-eight of them, on a day
when you were walking by the river not thinking
of anything, and suddenly there were ibises, not merely one or two,
but many – like the multitude we saw once,
unremarked as eleventh-century princes or the ghosts of princes,
stepping with hesitant elegance through a twenty-first-century scroll
of televised evening news, inserting precision beaks
into mounds of gaily coloured landfill, entering together
the art of the unknown because it is autumn
and the leaves are slicing the air, and because
they like to gather at this time of year – as we do,
meaning that among fifty-eight ibises and two people
there is always one who loves you, and that she is thinking
of ibises standing and grazing, all fifty-eight ibises
that you saw along the river that day, as she waits for you
with the leaves flying, now that it is autumn once more –
meaning that she who loves you, loves you.

A small town, built on pearling
and the button trade.

The red soil of the local cemetery
with its segregated divers' graves.

Paths come upon at the periphery
and walkable at low tide.

Not of tears then, but of oceans: pearl shell,
harvested by hand, by divers

strung on air lines walked across the sea floor,
not-yet-yellowed clippings marking three more

of the town's sons newly lost down there –
they drift off toward sleep, freed from that air.

Nacreous as in pearl shell, that is, not of tears,
of noctilucent clouds still forming just offshore,

nacre of oceans, calcium and rime. That pearly ore.
The mud flats, now that it is evening,

lit up underneath, sublunary, alluvial.
Faces and scenes, now only dimly seen,

reflected in the pearls you wear.
Old photos of the luggers and their gear,

the ancestors of those still living here.
A cardboard box holding the entrance fees,

and the old woman, half-asleep above it, at the door
to the dusty, tin-roofed museum that holds all that local history.

LEIGH BELLINGALL, OR SPRING

With blue flowers and with rain,
with irises and rivulets and chocolate fritillaria,
with rafters and lobelia and a sky-blue umbrella
unfurled in the bathtub alongside vases and jars
of many kinds of blue flowers, purple camas
and fringed black tulips, and with vase-shapes
prefigured in the tulips, like an old
Egyptian princess from the other world, she comes,
her umbrella dripping in the upstairs tub,
and drenched violets, and the light on,
and all that she has gathered, just to show
that she is with us, in her navy-blue raincoat
from an older world, and the window wide,
and the screen pulled up
for no apparent reason
other than air and rain
and a perfect lack of instruction,
with all these she comes.
I call her Leigh Bellingall
for a girl I knew once, though that
is not her proper name, like the stone on which
whole oceans and continents are seen jostling,
fix your eyes firmly, for you are
pulled apart by winds and she was here,
the window wide and the light left on,
that's how she appears at least,
stepping inside with mandatory flowers,
with jam jars of evening lobelia and funerary tulips,
in a blue raincoat from the other world,

appears and is gone, gone now, gone
with the leaves, with the blown-down leaves
in the yellow twilight and a light left on.

Every few years the old one breaks along its spine,
the pages come unstrung, and I'm obliged to buy a new one.
The Bs and Ms and Ss have been used up anyway, the older
crossed-out versions' various replacements creeping
backwards to encroach upon the As and Ls and Rs –
my friends move too often, leaving little room for newcomers.
And so, every few years, I'll pick a sunny afternoon
and sit down to the leisurely task of transferring
the names and details to the stiff new pages.
Each time, with some alarm, I come across a few
I find no face for any longer, no memory of meeting –
whatever common history must have once existed,
gone. With these I hesitate, then let them go,
and turn back to the rest. Among those I'll be taking
forward with me is a small (small, but slowly growing) number –
those whose phones no longer work, and to whom
mail is never delivered. When I come upon one of these,
each solitary and apart yet retaining perversely
its place in this alphabet, my pen stops a moment, as if on its own –
then (once more as if on its own) having been called back to its task,
starts up again, copying the obsolete details
very carefully into the new book.

Another dawn
another gift from the cat
glistening on the doorstep

Fine as a jeweller's drill
entering someone's sleep
the robin's song

An old board game
inventing new rules around missing pieces
(daylight moon)

Rescued from drowning
in the cream pitcher
the moth leaves behind some powder for the coffee of its rescuer

Summer at last and so the door left open
an earwig makes its way across the floorboards
apparently also invited

Home finally with his parting gift
the teacher looks into the face
of the freckled orchid

Bucket of sand clams on the counter
new blade
parting the shell and living meat

Thirty years spent in this house
(still learning
the names of all the neighbourhood cats)

Falling maple keys
so many doors to the windy mansion
and no one home

Which path
which path among the flowers
butterfly

Sometimes on a winter midnight I wake

to winterlight, and the past that isn't gone.
Driving in winter, two girls on our own.

Late – still only halfway through New Hampshire,
on our way to Maine. Stopping in ski country –

barely enough between us for a room –
amidst so many well-heeled strangers.

After the steep climb to the second floor,
the feel of being parachuted into sleep,

then, without warning, morning sun,
the new snow out the windows of the little inn.

Coffee, cornflakes and cream that came
free for the asking, before the breakfast order.

From there to here
it's one step, maybe two.

Making my way downstairs by winterlight,
a half-moon balanced in the pines.

The snow, the light from the snow,
is delicate, cold, dense, not deep.

Leaving the others
to cards
and sleep,
the spider
in the woodpile,
we've come,
following a
glimmer of trail,
roots, rocks
and darkness,
to lie down
looking up,
mid-August,
mid-August
wildfire in the sky.

Now that I've heard at least half my friends making love
(not all together, mind you) – passing a closed door in the hall,

through casually opened windows, or thin summer walls,
even amplified once – the pipe beside the stove

suddenly crying and grunting as I fried the eggs –
it's as if I'd dallied with them myself – a little wearily perhaps,

but after, knowing which one whimpers, whose fingers want to be licked.
And now that all, or most, are scattered, or else gone,

and the nights, empty of those sounds, grow long,
as long as those once but no more well-travelled highways stretched

across the plains, town after town with their motels strung
with post-Christmas lights still glistening in the rain –

now, now, what a strange joy it would be,
to hear those cries again, to once more breach that privacy.

Now all the griefs are done but one or two,
in the dregs, the dark days of December,
which month is all one room, which some
may never leave, whose needs have drifted
as the river's course might, and whose debts
are to be paid in flowers now – wild
mountain pinks for instance – paid in spring
then paid and paid again each year
as if such debts can never be
fully repaid or cancelled, but instead fuel
springtime's sweetest faintest scents.
Now all the griefs are gone, but for that one
or two, which can be neither – in the dark
days of December, between the solstice
and the year's end – done nor undone,
a time for clearing debts still not yet paid
and now only to be paid in kind –
whatever nurtures, gives, ends,
nourishing the spring to come.

Stealthy among mint
another winter squash unfurls
another of its flagrant yellow blossoms

By the time the moon has risen
the snail will have climbed
to the cut top
            of the central trunk
                        of the tall cedar

A plane burrowing into a cloud
all afternoon long
the phone doesn't ring

Bitter cool and sweet
the cucumbers' moonlight can't penetrate
once their cords are cut

Three a.m. the snarling squealing and simpering begins
raccoons cavorting among the vines
and the tomatoes aren't even ripe

It's possible to waste one's talents
in the echoing moonlight
to waste one's talents   in the echoing   moonlight

Courting the red trumpet flowers
hummingbirds in spring
in autumn bees and wasps

At last a ripe tomato
an earwig walking out of
the first love bite

A bell from the earth.
In summertime.
At dusk.
July.
An intimation,
or a warning,
only joyous,
not for this –
this moment,
but the next.
A proclamation –
of contingency –
to mark
not what is
certain, and yet
still to come,
but what might
yet be
brought forth
into being –
chanted by rote,
and in the dark,
the darker the louder,
almost in unison.
A bell
from the earth –
the ripple,
too,
of temporary quiet

radiated by
each footstep.
Overhead,
light cloud.
Few stars.
The first hard freeze
of August,
or October,
that will come
to silence them.

JOHN THOMPSON

– for Douglas Lochhead

Where did you go John Thompson? How did you get away?
With the spring light falling
and your eyes turned away. Like the light in the forest,
the trickle through the marshland of ice at midday.

Where did you go John Thompson? April, so much like fall
with the dead leaves underfoot and distant knock
of axe-fall. One night you set out
and by morning weren't anywhere at all.

THE INVENTION OF AUTUMN, LATE SEPTEMBER,
CANADIAN SHIELD

A single note in the monotonic scale,
and a plate slides shut in the earth.
Heard or not heard.

All the animals of summer,
everything now living,
halted, turned towards it.

Overhead the clouds revolve.

Unseen yet, autumn
inside them. An extra dimension
to be felt with this whole-body glove.

Another dawn
another gift from the cat

Fine as a jeweller's drill
the robin's song

An old board game, box taped up at its corners,
daylight moon among the missing pieces

A moth, rescued from drowning in the cream pitcher
summer at last

An earwig makes its way across the floorboards
sand clams on the counter

Home with his parting gift, the teacher
looking once more into the freckled orchid's face

Thirty years spent living in this house
so many doors, so many falling maple keys

Which path then before evening
which path among the flowers' butterflies

BROOME, NOT LONG NOW UNTIL DUSK, THINKING OF LI BAI'S "SITTING ALONE AT JINGTING MOUNTAIN"

A small town built on pearling and the button trade.
Descendants of those laid out in the red soil of the local cemetery's
segregated divers' graves, now, towards day's end,
sat on lawn chairs, barbecuing on the local green,
its view out to the bay and sunset still to come.
Paths come upon at the periphery, and walkable at low tide.
Crabs of all sizes climbing in and out, down there
among the mangroves. Plummeting seeds, bombs, keys,
arboreal armies marching into the sea.
Pearls from the Dampier Peninsula for sale
for sale for sale for sale the whole length of the street.
'Pearl meat' on a white plate, served up in a hollowed
ice-cave at the local Thai café, this made (according to the waiter)
by submerging a balloon in water in a small container,
capped somehow, and placed into a freezer at the back.
Coming back, after the long day,
to the small motel, the room that looks out (almost) over Roebuck Bay.
The room's two live-in geckos, companionable, quick,
appearing suddenly along the sofa back.
They look back peaceably,
the two of them, and never tire,
watching me as I drift off towards sleep.

Out of the ordinariness of the day,
a dog comes trotting, stops and shakes
himself, and the leash that fastens him
less to the one who holds it than to the plan
for the afternoon: an hour of varied winds
that stop and start in the mind of April,
and the leash, and the man to walk with,
and a woman who passes,
whose ordinary mood is dispelled
by a dog that wags its tail in a body-wide
smile of unpartitionable joy,
sun and petals awry,
and her hair blown wildly by the wind,
on the northeast corner of Marlee and Eglinton.

SMALL HORSE

Small horse walking out of a flower,
what business do you have in this world?
Small horse amidst the regiments of horses,
soldiers, beings of steel,
mayfly or June bug,
what kind of thing are you,
wearing the colours of July –
what precisely is your business here,
smallish one?
Why do you walk toward me out of a flower
at this late hour?

SUMAC, WEED PATH, LILAC

When this is gone, all gone to dust,
house, land, home, all this property,
whatever's missed, those things we touched,
sumac, brick, weed path, lilac, we
may not remember, or they us,
being, in that diminished state, not much
of anything, just atoms, lees,
lesser powders, nibbled crusts –
then some stray wind may lift, meddle
the dust, loss, crumbs, old curled leaves;
sweep, sift, soften, plane, and settle;
build; plaster; plant; invite the cats, who'll come,
find what is new, and someone's, and be gone.

Hiss of warning from the cattails
weapons drawn suddenly
one among the month's blue cornflowers trod on in the grass

Silvery by the bedside
a money spider
and an upside-down wine carafe

Among huckleberry brush the rain ends
how many mirrored worlds collide
then at a touch slurred wetness

Trailing petals front door to kitchen
kitchen back to front door
some kind of vanishing act

In the morning sky's deep evening-blue
New York   Delhi   Khartoum
suburbs of the moon

Damp earth moss and fern
five p.m. in winter
here where I was born

Once the lights are out
moonlight returns
to this its former home

Berkeley in drizzle, still –
two deer materialize
an old mirror hanging in the hall

LINES WRITTEN AFTER READING SHAW NEILSON

Say hello to summer when I've gone,
to the hawthorn, and ornamental apple,
all that hapless pink, to the delicate
lace-winged couple on the window screen,
the breeze which, being migratory,
leaves for now, returning when it will.
Also to migrating fish,
the red-winged blackbird on its reedy stilt,
the leaves, all ears, emerging from the stem,
that do not fully die
and hence may rise again.

In the long low northern darkness where it's dusk
all day and no spring comes, only a faint gold colour,
blackbirds and jackdaws, the raked graves –
this is the beginning, or else the end of sorrow,
wheels clutching at wheels, wayward among stones.
There are places on earth the soul must appear,
and others it shies away from, but here, neither,
never, nor, and no spring comes, only trowels
and turnings and wheelbarrows full of flowers,
the jackdaws hopping across the straightened graves –
no spring comes to the long low country
where the body is made to lie, only the faint gold
of a winter's noon or the midnight sky, midsummer
midnight, and the small fires, laid out along
the shores, sounds, sands, and narrows of that country.

My grandfather died yesterday,
in the evening. He wanted
nothing done about his death, no fuss.
For him, death was nothing special.

If I'm lucky, that attitude
will have been passed down to me.
Somewhere in my body, a column
of figures is being added up
and a new sum arrived at.

For now, the family does not join hands,
though it is joined by blood. My father,
in his chair, has nodded off again,
and so is lost to sleep.

A reading lamp burns on above him.

From what I have gathered in his garden,
I would like to lay this wreath at his feet.

CEDARVALE

DIARY

Early winter, post-solstice, and the mind is already turning toward things that are not yet before the eyes, looking forward to another repetition and variation on the sights of past springs:

> A robin
> almost too heavy
> for the cherry twig –

It's possible to acquire a catalogue of such things – settings-out, things seen – without knowing whether or not these constitute a continuing reality, or merely carry within them the stamp of some expired, transfiguring, imperative. Always the flavour of a given life, both evanescent and repeatable. On the verge of entering another new year, my sixtieth, something new has been added, a sense of the penultimate.

> Is it still blowing?
> That old wind
> old wind from long ago –

Not yet the ultimate, a little short of that.

A warm south wind has been blowing for two days now, and this is the result: 12 degrees Celsius. This is the weather of the west coast, not Ontario January, yet here it is. The ravine today is filled with a perfectly even mist, all the way to the tops of the trees. On my way home I ran into a woman I recognized, having met her once before, her and her small caramel-coloured dog. The path was mostly puddle, with a narrow raised strip, so I gestured for her to go first. Happy New Year, she said, and I asked if her dog thought it would be a good year too. She said yes. She said every year has the likelihood of being good when it first arrives. I said I felt this year *would* be a good one, though I hoped it was not just the weather today. (The forecast was for the cold north wind to return.) We live in hope, she said. And one after the other, woman and dog, both of them unfailingly polite, made their way along the narrow raised strip and continued on into the mist.

It is nearly twenty-five years since we moved into this house, which is near Cedarvale Ravine. First though, before moving in, we had to make our way by bus and then on foot through the biggest blizzard of the year to a far northern suburb where one of the children of the original owners now lived, to sign the contract that would make the house our own. It's a place that freezes in winter and boils in summer. Where the branches of the neighbour's backyard cherry trees extend over the fence and well into our own. In springtime the blossoms float like seafoam; on rainy summer days the entire world is lit with green leaves and darkening cherries; in autumn I watch a few more of the yellowing leaves drop to the grass, leaving behind yet another painting in the air. More than two decades have passed, and those trees still anchor us here, but now they have companions as well: a half-wild cherry in our yard, and two more young cherry trees in the yard of our neighbour on the other side, so that at the peak of blossoming the three houses are joined in a single vision. Or, as now, joined in a world of snow.

A flock of those little boat-shaped birds that always seem to go about in groups, blue-brown above, white below the curved "waterline." In a snow-laden crotch of the cherry tree, one of them will suddenly bow, eating the snow, sipping the snow. At the same time I've just discovered how those "snaky tunnels" are made – by squirrels, apparently at play. One just "jump-tobogganed" through the foot-high snow, leaving a sunken zigzag channel three inches deep the whole length of the yard.

The same three squirrels I've often seen chasing one another, their early morning silhouettes, following one another along the curving roads of branches until they disappear beyond a neighbour's roof, are here again. Calm winds, summer-like, in deepest winter: minus 25, and sunshine. Like memory itself, which brings things forth in the wrong season. Another kind of small bird, brown with white chevron-like flashes on its tail, sports playfully, landing every few seconds, bathing in the powdery snow as if it were a spring puddle. Every few seconds, another of these takes a turn splashing in the frozen landscape.

So many tracks in the snow, going this way and that: squirrel, bird, cat. Soon the apricot-grey haze of the city will glow between bare branches; above the downtown towers a yellowing moon will float up, fragile and ancient. Soon I'll be following two ski tips, skimming along the ravine at dusk, keeping to the pale track, almost phosphorescent, of the skier who went before.

Today we saw a big hawk devouring what looked like a bluebird in our backyard, under the bare branches of the lilac. This went on for about an hour, until Kim could hold off no longer, and started shovelling snow, at which point the hawk listened carefully for about ten minutes, then took off with what was left of its prey. Later I went out and with the toe of my boot scuffed clean snow over the pinkish snow, burying along with it the few blue-grey feathers that were left behind.

This winter has brought a preponderance of cardinals. It's common to see three or four at once through the back windows, flitting here and there. Kim makes a distinction between the males and females, referring to them as either Richelieus or Claudias. Just now two Richelieus and two Claudias, four altogether, are in the bare grey lilac. Beside the sumac, with its forty or fifty reddish seed clusters like standing flames. Big flakes of snow are making their wandery way down along the twisting currents, volatile air, and it occurs to me that this is precisely the life I would have chosen had I been offered it at the age of fifteen or sixteen or seventeen, when I had no idea how to meet the future, and spent much of my time (unsuccessfully) trying to imagine it into being.

In the snow-fringed yard, a young squirrel, hopping *straight* into the air. Once, twice, a third time.

> The sadness of things that leave the world,
> the happiness of things still coming into being –

This young squirrel, so obviously excited by life, makes me ashamed of the sombre thoughts that have preoccupied me, on and off, for much of the winter. Once, when I was well into my thirties, a favourite aunt, who is dead now, accused me of being *too young to appreciate a kitten*. At the time I felt only the slight sting of what seemed an obscure (and in truth rather peculiar) insult. Now perhaps I begin to know what she meant. Six or seven robins are congregated along the path that leads, a scant block from the house, into the ravine. Last night it rained, and the puddles are filled to brimming with large pinky-brown worms, more bare than bare, exciting the robins' expectations. Each year a similar troop of robins appears at this spot: heralds, messengers from afar, bringing with them another spring.

The snow is gone from the streets, but in the ravine freshets of snow-melt still run along either side of the path where the ground is lowest. One toy boat-hull or miniature barge of snow, foamy-looking, weightless, like styrofoam. A piece of bark makes its way down one of these freshets, spinning, pirouetting over the "rapids," then gets stuck, like another toy boat, all on its own. On the shady side, scalloped ice-terraces that will melt by late afternoon.

The robins return first, then the shrill of the first returning red-winged blackbird is heard, and not long afterwards the red-headed woodpecker is drilling into the neighbour's cherry trees. A pair of cardinals has spent much of two days apparently trying to get into the house, flying at the windows on the west side, where an eastern white cedar grows. The cedar's branches touch the windows, and in storms make squeaking noises scraping back and forth across the glass. The cardinals flutter at the window on the ground floor, then hover against the upstairs windows, looking in, as though to spy a nest site indoors. After several tries they give up, fly off to the backyard for a brief rest. A cardinal in the backyard sumac – as Kim says – like a temporary sumac bud. Again and again they return to the windows, as though to a problem that can be solved only by endless repetition.

The cardinals have been at it every day for a week now. One after the other they try flying against the windows, standing vertically as it were in the air, beaks hitting the panes. From another room it sounds as though a large bee were striking the glass again and again. Clapping doesn't dissuade them, or at least not for long. The male is a deep red, the female dun and blush-coloured, and she is the more fanatical of the two. The cedar tree, so close to the house, provides a close-up view of the squirrels and birds all year round, and is maybe a partial contributor to what seems a category confusion on the part of this pair of cardinals. Could it be that the branches appear multiplied in the windows – as though a whole forest were standing in the place of a single tree? The male makes a beautiful song, even in his frustration.

The first pale blossoms on the apples in the ravine, apparently frail, yet not: these trees have stood along the path for far longer than I've lived here. Some of the trees are highly perfumed – the pinker the blossom, the more delectable the scent. It's the same with the fruit: an apple with a blush tastes sweeter. Thoreau wrote: "I would have my thoughts, like wild apples, to be food for walkers, and will not warrant them to be palatable if tasted in the house." In fact he left his last works to fall only after his passing, like windfall apples, sure and sweet. Others happened along and sorted them, editing them posthumously, until at last someone published the whole as *Wild Fruits*, my favourite among his books because it is the least *worked*. The house is of course the place I like best to contemplate his thoughts; out walking, there are blossoms and fruits to consider, of the sorts that can't be found in books. Someone I fell into casual conversation with today, near those apple trees, told me that cardinals quite often fly against windowpanes, attacking the image of what seems to them an enemy, reflected in the glass. A simple explanation, but is it true? And now the rustle of rain. Rain coming down, the sky sliding east with the clouds.

> In a second-storey room
> to sleep
> among the blossoms –

Yesterday afternoon the first few blossoms opened on the small cherry in our yard. Not in the morning, but by afternoon they could hold out no longer. This is the tree our neighbours planted for us as a surprise one year when we were away. Later they apologized, saying it was the "wrong kind" of cherry. But in fact, though its fruit is small, the flavour is unequalled. We've always supposed that the grafted part failed, leaving the wild cherry to grow as it might, straight from the roots. And today, right on time, the first bumblebee.

> Assailed in the night by wind and rain
> don't the blossoms love it this morning
> their wild roots wet

Looking out the dining room window early in the morning I find that someone is in the backyard – bent over, stooping and moving on, stooping and moving on. It's a middle-aged woman I've never laid eyes on before. She doesn't even glance in my direction – though I'm framed in the window behind her – but holds a garden fork of some kind, and a plastic bag, which, I now see, she is filling with not-yet-flowering dandelion greens. She keeps this up for a good ten minutes, then departs with her haul, never once having turned to look at me.

We go for a ravine walk with our friend from Wuhan, who shows us a game from his childhood.

> Pulling a new spray of willow through his teeth
> he shows how it's done:
> making a "rat's tail" –

How quickly they're gone, these days, blown away on the breeze. Yet in the house, time and heat are already beginning to pile up. Spring pressing in from all sides.

Cedarvale Ravine. The female horsetails are thick in the marshy, boggy places, and along the thin wash of creek. More red-winged blackbirds now, in the stand of last year's cattails, new shoots of cattail sprouting alongside.

> Everything rain-washed
> wind-washed
> standing that much taller today

The blackbirds punctuating the air with regular clock-like trills.

Deep in the ravine last week, one morning, a police car and paramedics van, with five or six emergency crew in their reflective yellow vests. I passed right by on the narrow path, averting my eyes. A thin man lay on a stretcher. Later that day, there was no sign that hell had visited, just as there's no reminder now of the apples' blossoming. All of nature is a kind of subtraction, with nothing left over: whatever we see, whatever we think is there, is then wholly gone, wholly changed into something other.

A white-haired woman was gathering a huge bouquet of wildflowers, which I stopped to admire. It turned out the bouquet was a gift for her friend – one of those who'd helped "save" Cedarvale Ravine. Decades ago, she explained, when the city was planning an expressway, a few of the women from the neighbourhood had come together to present their views at city hall. There were now only two left, out of the original group. The idea had been this: each of them had a large house and garden, but for those who lived in apartments, with no hope of a garden, there was only this ravine, and thus the plan had been to preserve a piece of wild garden for everyone. Not a year ago, on the other hand, I came upon a man who had just finished digging up a particularly striking shrub, taking for himself what had grown wild here, for transplanting to his own garden.

A young snake has been dipped in white paint, so it writhes along the ravine path, trying to escape its own skin, suffocating. The two boys who have done this (telltale paint can in hand) startle when they see me coming. How would you like somebody to do that to you, I yell, and they scramble off into the woods.

The cherries are ripe. Robins come to eat them, two birds on a single branch. The larger bird pecks first at the ripest cherry within reach; as soon as the other bird tries, it too is pecked! The larger one alternates between pecking at the cherries and pecking at the other bird, keeping that one from managing even a single bite.

At night the gangs of raccoons comb through the neighbourhood, making their strange whoops and trills. My neighbour, leaning out from her porch, makes kissing noises, calling in the cat.

> Washing my hair
> wringing it out with one hand
> moonrise

The next morning she says something has been at her lettuces. What sort of thing? "A white animal," she replies, and makes the sign for "fangs" with her two index fingers. Could it be a possum?

Midsummer in the ravine. Where a makeshift bridge of two boards crosses the creek, yellow flags bloom shoulder-high, tresses of dark jade cress blowing in the water, anchored in silt. Two women, dressed (impossibly) in kimono – mother and daughter? aunt and niece? – bend midstream, ankle-deep, gathering handfuls into plastic supermarket bags. They would make a graceful subject for a nineteenth-century Japanese woodblock print. I can hardly believe my eyes, yet a few days later I glimpse them again, dressed in ordinary shirts and pants this time, crouched well off the path, on the soft muddy ground among the lily stalks, each wielding a small stubby knife. What could they be collecting? Lily buds? Lily bulbs?

The house never gives up its heat willingly, but stores it up from day to day, until it rains.

> Years of summers:
> a trunk so full of rocks and shells
> it won't be budged –

After the rain, the entire neighbourhood stands steaming in the sunshine.

The longed-for hard rains have come, and all at once the roof is leaking. "Animal damage" is the verdict, meaning the squirrels have pried up the shingles, preparing to make a winter nest in the attic. First we had to have that portion of the roof re-shingled, then trim back the cedar tree that allowed such easy access. A trio of men arrived. One hauled himself up into the tree with a loop of rope, another handed him the chainsaw, and he began to cut a "hole" in the foliage so that he could throw the branches and small trash out through it onto the front lawn. Next he took out one of the two secondary trunks, and then the other. Finally he hopped down and sawed the smaller branches from the cut trunks. One of the other men started feeding the smaller branches into the chipper at the back of their truck. The two trunks were cut into shorter sections, and I asked the men to take them round the back, and watched as they dropped them into the grass. Later Kim came home and wrapped the long pile in black plastic, so that it could weather over the winter, and perhaps eventually be made into garden stakes. Together the trunk sections make a body nearly the size and shape of a man. The birds avoided the tree all day; then late in the day one came, stood on one of the bare cut trunks, and screeched repeatedly. No one came or answered. And that was the end of our idyll of the birds and squirrels.

Late-summer jaunts through the ravine are pleasantly uneventful, which is to say they are improvised of events too numerous and subtle to detail. Always I take stock, in a sweeping way, of the minutely altering complexion of the weeds, trees, and grasses: which patches are in bud, or in bloom, or fading. And then today, out of nowhere, another sort of weather entirely: a pastoral of heavy mist. Two half-bald men, in sagging shirts and trousers, knee-deep in the damp grasses, chatting to one another. But what is it they stoop to gather from the matted weeds, among moth-eaten cattails, sodden purple asters? Something round, each no bigger than a quarter, dozens of them bulging the white plastic sacks they are carrying. I stop to ask. "Very expensive!" cries one of the men, and holds out his palm: snail. I nod, and wave, turning from the lovely tiger-striped shell pulled from its home in the weeds, and head back through the coolness of a foreign mist.

At times, when I think I'm done with looking, I crawl into bed and close my eyes, and there before me once again is the very world I closed my eyes to.

> End of autumn cricket
> my hearing too
> grows faint

This house came into being in the same year Kim did, which endears it to me doubly. From its windows can be seen the autumn leaves, which are at their peak now, crimson and scarlet and burnt sienna. At the end of my sixth decade of life it dawns on me that I've been granted an extension – as a different sort of creature. What is this creature with the old eyes? Increasingly girlish, liking anew the old girlish things. Chocolate; lace; lying down to watch the clouds scudding past, the blue October sky . . .

Early morning, sun just up, late autumn. A sudden snow surprises the sparrows and willows.

The feral cats of the neighbourhood have been many over the years; they come and go; die and are born. One such cat – big, with matted long fur and wild green intelligent dreamy eyes – used to spend a great deal of time in our yard, resting in the morning and again at evening beneath the lilac tree by the back fence. We used to see him there, crouched in the snow after his exploits or stretched out in the sunshine, warming himself, afraid of no one. After not seeing him at all for several months, we wondered if even he had finally met his end. But no – a woman from the apartment building two doors down had taken him in, and from that time on he has no longer cared to venture out, having entered the ease of his retirement. This is the same woman who once, when telling me about another matter – a local cat who'd been cruelly deformed by a wire trap – began by patiently explaining, "I was busy setting out some peanut butter sandwiches for the squirrels, when . . ."

When it snows it snows equally on what is left of the living cedar in the front yard and the lengths of cut cedar wrapped in black plastic in the backyard. When the snow melts from the plastic, one of the cardinals likes to sit there in the sun, where the winter warmth is gathered and stored. Cardinals and bluebirds are the birds I drew when I was a child, thinking them exotic, copying their colours and forms from pictures in books, and now, quite by chance, I live among them. In the ravine, bent stalks serve as half-woven basketry for the snow; in the half-distance, the beautiful brown architecture of the woods. An album of days. It may be that in the future no one will think of gathering snails from the weeds, or cress from the creek, or set out peanut butter sandwiches for the squirrels.

> In the quiet before snow
> the book is not its words
> the cats are lovely and stubborn –

This place, such as it has been, will truly be gone from the world. Something else will have taken its place. Where else would lost things be found then, but in the words that once stood for them?

NOTES AND ACKNOWLEDGEMENTS

"Painted Garden" is for Janice Gurney, Andy Patton, and Kim Maltman. Janice made her find (a fragment clearly marked as being from the reign of Marcus Aurelius) while participating in an archaeological dig atop Monte Testaccio, an artificial hill forty-five storeys high composed principally of broken shards of ancient olive oil amphorae. The Baths of Caracalla are the ruins of the grand, or possibly grandiose, public baths built during the reign of the Roman emperor Caracalla. The equestrian statue of Marcus Aurelius, known to posterity as the "last good emperor," can be seen in the Capitoline Museum. The basilica San Miniato al Monte commands an outstanding view over the city of Florence and beyond.

"Mothlight" is for André Alexis, and takes inspiration from his libretto for "Moths: A Song Cycle," a collaboration with composer James Rolfe.

"Putting a Seal on Speech and an End to Wandering": The City History Museum in the Plaça del Rei in Barcelona, in addition to containing items detailing a past stretching from prehistory to the present, sits atop an underground complex of variously excavated streets, housing, implements, and the like, the whole providing a glimpse of life in Roman times, when the city was called Barcino. Only a few steps away, a plaque marks the site where Christopher Columbus is said to have presented himself to King Ferdinand and Queen Isabella on returning from his first voyage to the New World.

"Meteor-Watching with Cameron" is for Cameron Hayne.

"John Thompson" is in memory of Douglas Lochhead.

Thanks to the Canada Council for the Arts, to the Ontario Arts Council, and to the following: *Arc Poetry Magazine, Brick: A Literary Journal,* Brick Books, and Wolsak & Wynn Publishers Ltd., for much-appreciated support. Thanks also to the editors of *Arc Poetry Magazine, The Malahat Review,* and *The Warwick Review,* in which versions of some of the poems first appeared.

Finally, thanks to Ken Babstock for a new perspective; to Anita Chong, Paul Eprile, and Heather Sangster; and to Kim Maltman, for literary collaboration from start to finish.